Sports Illustrated KIDS

W9-CMN-561

THE ULTIMATE GUIDE TO PRO BASKETBALL TEAMS

by Nate LeBoutillier

CAPSTONE PRESS
a capstone imprint

Sports Illustrated KIDS Ultimate Pro Team Guides are published
by Capstone Press, 151 Good Counsel Drive, P.O. Box 669,
Mankato, Minnesota 56002. www.capstonepub.com

Printed in the United States of America
in North Mankato, Minnesota.

032010
005740CGF10

Library of Congress Cataloging-in-Publication Data
LeBoutillier, Nate.
  The ultimate guide to pro basketball teams / by Nate LeBoutillier.
    p. cm.—(Sports Illustrated KIDS. Ultimate pro guides)
Includes index.
ISBN 978-1-4296-4821-9 (library binding)
ISBN 978-1-4296-5641-2 (paperback)
  1. National Basketball Association—Juvenile literature.
  2. Basketball teams—United States—Juvenile literature.
  3. Basketball teams—Ontario—Toronto—Juvenile literature.
  I. Title. II. Series.
GV885.515.N37L43 2011
  796.323'64—dc22   2010012057

Editorial Credits: Anthony Wacholtz, editor; Tracy Davies, designer;
Eric Gohl, media researcher; Laura Manthe, production specialist

Image Credits: Dreamstime: Alexandre Fagundes De Fagundes, 44 (t);
iStockphoto: Bill Grove (basketball court), cover, back cover, 2, 66–67, 68–69,
70, 72; Newscom: 53 (b), 57 (t), 65 (b), AFP/Tony Ranze, 49 (b), Icon SMI/
Cliff Welch, 7 (t), Icon SMI/Mark Goldman, 64 (t); Shutterstock: Aprilphoto
(basketball), cover, back cover, 1, 68, doodle (shattered glass), back cover, 68,
Juampi Rodriguez, cover (bl), Michael Shake (basketball hoop), cover, Tomasz
Sowinski, design element; Sports Illustrated: Al Tielemans, 6 (b), 10 (t), 50 (t),
51 (t), Andy Hayt, 19 (t), 31 (all), 55 (t), Bill Frakes, 10 (b), 18 (t), 33 (b), Bob
Rosato, 6 (t), 7 (b), 14 (t), 17 (b), 20 (t), 30 (t), 34 (b), 35 (b), 38 (b), 43 (b), 48
(t), 49 (t), 59 (b), 62 (b), 66 (background middle), Damian Strohmeyer, cover
(br), 9 (b), 12 (t), 66 (front), David E. Klutho, 26 (t), 38 (t), 46 (t), 47 (b), 60
(t), 61 (b), Heinz Kluetmeier, 37 (t), Jeffery A. Salter, 11 (b), John Biever, cover
(bm), 13 (all), 14 (b), 23 (t), 32 (b), 36 (t), 63 (t), 66 (background right), John
D. Hanlon, 28 (b), 41 (b), 45 (b), John G. Zimmerman, 23 (b), John Iacono, 18
(b), John W. McDonough, 1, 2, 4–5, 8 (t), 11 (t), 15 (t), 16 (all), 17 (t), 19 (b),
22 (all), 24 (all), 28 (t), 29 (all), 30 (b), 32 (t), 33 (t), 34 (t), 35 (t), 36 (b), 40 (b),
42 (all), 47 (t), 52 (all), 53 (t), 54 (all), 56 (all), 58 (all), 59 (t), 61 (t), 62 (t), 63
(b), 66 (background left), 67 (all), Manny Millan, 12 (b), 15 (b), 20 (b), 21 (all),
25 (all), 26 (b), 27 (all), 40 (t), 41 (b), 43 (t), 44 (b), 45 (b), 46 (b), 48 (b), 50 (b),
51 (b), 60 (b), Richard Meek, 8 (b), Robert Beck, 39 (all), 57 (b), Simon Bruty,
64 (b), Walter Iooss Jr., 9 (t), 37 (b), 55 (b), 65 (t).

TABLE OF CONTENTS

Hoops on the Hardwood...........................4
Atlanta Hawks....................................6
Boston Celtics...................................8
Charlotte Bobcats...............................10
Chicago Bulls...................................12
Cleveland Cavaliers.............................14
Dallas Mavericks................................16
Denver Nuggets..................................18
Detroit Pistons.................................20
Golden State Warriors...........................22
Houston Rockets.................................24
Indiana Pacers..................................26
Los Angeles Clippers............................28
Los Angeles Lakers..............................30
Memphis Grizzlies...............................32
Miami Heat......................................34
Milwaukee Bucks.................................36
Minnesota Timberwolves..........................38
New Jersey Nets.................................40
New Orleans Hornets.............................42
New York Knicks.................................44
Oklahoma City Thunder...........................46
Orlando Magic...................................48
Philadelphia 76ers..............................50
Phoenix Suns....................................52
Portland Trail Blazers..........................54
Sacramento Kings................................56
San Antonio Spurs...............................58
Toronto Raptors.................................60
Utah Jazz.......................................62
Washington Wizards..............................64

Team Map..68
Glossary..70
Basketball Positions............................70
Read More.......................................71
Internet Sites..................................71
Index...72

HOOPS ON THE HARDWOOD

IN December 1891 physical education teacher James Naismith from Springfield, Massachusetts, was presented with a challenge. He was asked to come up with a new game that could be played during the cold New England winters. The result was basket ball—a game where two teams tried to toss a soccer ball into peach baskets nailed to the wall at opposite ends of the room.

Flash forward to the 1950s, when Bob Cousy of the Boston Celtics and Bob Pettit of the St. Louis Hawks scored with one-handed shots. In the 1960s giant centers Bill Russell of the Celtics and Wilt Chamberlain of the Philadelphia Warriors battled under

the rim. Pete Maravich of the New Orleans Jazz and Julius Erving of the Philadelphia 76ers thrilled fans in the 1970s. Larry Bird of the Celtics and Magic Johnson of the Los Angeles Lakers rose to championship levels in the 1980s. In the 1990s Michael Jordan put on a display, helping the Chicago Bulls win six championships.

Today basketball rivals soccer as the world's most-played game. In the United States, the National Basketball Association is the sport's professional organization. With such stars as Kobe Bryant, LeBron James, and Dwight Howard lighting up the court, basketball fans will always be at the edges of their seats.

ATLANTA HAWKS

First Season: 1949–1950

Franchise Record: 2,376–2,454
Home Arena: Phillips Arena
(18,729 capacity) in Atlanta, Georgia

CHAMPIONSHIP
1958

One of the NBA's original teams, the franchise got its start in 1949. The Tri-Cities Blackhawks were based in the Tri-Cities area of Moline and Rock Island, Illinois, and Davenport, Iowa. Two years later the team moved to Milwaukee and shortened its name to the Hawks. In 1955 the Hawks relocated to St. Louis. There they captured their first and only NBA title in 1958 behind their first star, Bob Pettit. The Hawks moved once more in 1968 to Atlanta, where they have been ever since.

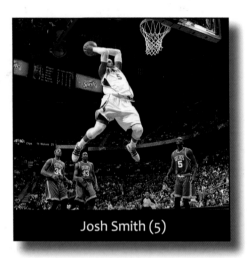
Josh Smith (5)

Legends & Stars

Joe Johnson (2)

Lou Hudson	G/F	1966–1977	"Sweet Lou" was a solid point guard and a six-time All-Star
Joe Johnson	G	2005–present	The tall guard can cut to the rim or rain in three-pointers
Pete Maravich	G	1970–1974	In 1970–1971 "Pistol Pete" averaged 23.2 points as a rookie
Dikembe Mutombo	C	1996–2001	"Mount Mutombo" led the NBA in rebounds in three of his four-plus seasons as a Hawk
Bob Pettit	F/C	1954–1965	The hustling, workhorse forward was the 1954–1955 Rookie of the Year and the NBA's MVP in 1956 and 1959
Josh Smith	F	2004–present	Amazing jumping ability makes Smith a rim-rocking, shot-blocking superstar
Dominique Wilkins	G/F	1982–1994	The "Human Highlight Film" was a great scorer and an incredible dunker

By the Numbers

POINTS	**Dominique Wilkins** 1982–1994 23,292	**STEALS**	**Mookie Blaylock** 1992–1999 1,321
REBOUNDS	**Bob Pettit** 1954–1965 12,849	**BLOCKS**	**Tree Rollins** 1977–1988 2,283
ASSISTS	**Glenn "Doc" Rivers** 1983–1991 3,866	**THREES**	**Mookie Blaylock** 1,050

Hawks of War

The Atlanta Hawks got their name from their ancestors, the Tri-Cities Blackhawks. The Tri-Cities are located where the Black Hawk War was fought in 1832. The war pitted Sac and Fox Indians led by tribal chief Black Hawk against the U.S. Army and state militia. Future President Abraham Lincoln and future Confederate President Jefferson Davis served during the war. Though the NBA team eventually relocated to Atlanta, the name stuck.

Al Horford (15), 2008 playoffs

Return to the Playoffs

In the 2007–2008 season, the Hawks returned to the NBA playoffs after an eight-season playoff drought, the longest in franchise history. In their return the Hawks nearly upset the eventual NBA-champion Boston Celtics, but lost the series in seven games.

BOSTON CELTICS

First Season: 1946–1947

Franchise Record: 2,972–2,031
Home Arena: TD Banknorth Garden
(18,624 capacity) in Boston, Massachusetts

CHAMPIONSHIPS

1957, 1959, 1960, 1961, 1962, 1963, 1964, 1965, 1966, 1968, 1969, 1974, 1976, 1981, 1984, 1986, 2008

The Celtics, one of the NBA's three oldest teams, are the most successful NBA franchise. The team has won 17 championships dating back to 1957. They continued to dominate the court in the 1960s, winning nine of the decade's championships behind center Bill Russell. The Celtics added two more titles in the 1970s and three in the 1980s, thanks largely to the clutch play of forward Larry Bird. In 2008 the Celtics returned to glory by winning it all for the first time in 22 seasons.

2008 NBA champions

Legends & Stars

★★★

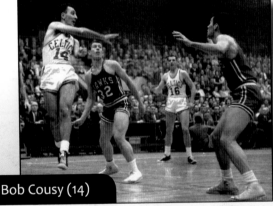
Bob Cousy (14)

Larry Bird	F	1979–1992	Considered one of the best players of all time, Bird received three consecutive MVPs and led the Celtics to three titles
Bob Cousy	G	1950–1963	The "Houdini of the Hardwood" ran the show with flair, winning six NBA titles and a place in the Hall of Fame
John Havlicek	G/F	1962–1978	"Hondo" was selected to 13 straight All-Star games
Robert Parish	C	1980–1994	A nine-time All-Star, "Chief" patrolled the paint in Boston for 14 of his all-time record 21 NBA seasons
Paul Pierce	F	1998–present	"The Truth" led the Celtics to the NBA title in 2008
Rajon Rondo	G	2006–present	Rising point guard played in his first All-Star Game in 2010
Bill Russell	C	1956–1969	The five-time MVP was a defensive and rebounding whiz

By the Numbers

POINTS
John Havlicek
1962–1978
26,395

REBOUNDS
Bill Russell
1956–1969
21,620

ASSISTS
Bob Cousy
1950–1963
6,945

STEALS
Larry Bird ⟶
1979–1992
1,556

BLOCKS
Robert Parish
1980–1994
1,703

THREES
Paul Pierce
1998–present
1,467

Pick a Number

The Celtics have retired 22 jerseys in their 63-year history. The number of retired jerseys is more than any other franchise in the NBA. Strangely, none of the retired numbers are in the 40s or 50s.

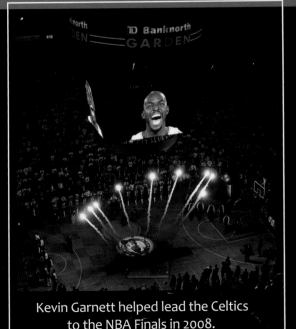

Kevin Garnett helped lead the Celtics to the NBA Finals in 2008.

From Second-Worst to First

On February 11, 2007, the Boston Celtics visited Minneapolis, Minnesota, to take on Kevin Garnett and the Timberwolves. The Celtics lost 109-107 on a last-second shot to lose their 18th straight game, a franchise record. It was a low point in a season where they finished as the NBA's second-worst team with a 24–58 record. But an offseason trade brought Garnett to Boston, and Ray Allen came over from the Seattle SuperSonics. The trades set the tone for a historic turnaround the next season. The Celtics finished a league-best 66–16 that year, capturing the 2008 NBA crown.

CHARLOTTE BOBCATS

First Season: 2004–2005

Franchise Record: 188–304

Home Arena: Time Warner Cable Arena
(19,026 capacity) in Charlotte, North Carolina

CHAMPIONSHIPS
None

Charlotte first became home to an NBA team in 1988 when the city was awarded an expansion franchise, the Hornets. But after 14 fairly successful seasons in Charlotte, the Hornets moved to New Orleans. In 2004 the NBA came calling again, this time granting Charlotte the expansion Bobcats.

The Bobcats' mascot, Rufus

Legends & Stars

Gerald Wallace

Raymond Felton	G	2005–present	The leading assist and three-point shooting man in Bobcat history continues to run the show in Charlotte
Gerald Henderson	G	2009–present	An explosive young scorer has the skill and the bloodlines—his father played in the NBA for 13 years—to succeed
Emeka Okafor	C/F	2004–2009	The franchise's first NBA draft pick was a hard-working battler who excelled in rebounding on both ends of the floor
Gerald Wallace	F	2004–present	The slashing guard shows no fear when driving to the hoop or playing tough defense

By the Numbers

POINTS	**Gerald Wallace** 2004–present 6,688	
REBOUNDS	**Emeka Okafor** 2004–2009 3,516	
ASSISTS	**Raymond Felton** 2005–present 2,573	
STEALS	**Gerald Wallace** 768	
BLOCKS	**Emeka Okafor** 621	
THREES	**Raymond Felton** 375 ⟶	

Terrific Turnaround

After five seasons with losing records, the Bobcats turned it around in 2009–2010. Behind the play of Gerald Wallace, Raymond Felton, and newly acquired Stephen Jackson, Charlotte finished with a winning regular-season record (44–38). It was the first time the young team made the playoffs.

Robert Johnson

Bobcat Billionaire

When Robert Johnson became the first African-American billionaire in 2000, it wasn't long before he decided to buy an NBA team. In 2002 Johnson put up the majority of the money to buy the franchise promised to the city of Charlotte after its previous NBA team, the Hornets, moved to New Orleans. Johnson, the founder of Black Entertainment Television (BET), went on to become the first black owner of a team in North American professional sports. In 2010 he sold the team to former NBA star Michael Jordan.

CHICAGO BULLS

Franchise Record: 1,818–1,757
Home Arena: United Center
(20,917 capacity) in Chicago, Illinois

CHAMPIONSHIPS
1991, 1992, 1993, 1996, 1997, 1998

First Season: 1966–1967

As the Midwest's largest city, Chicago was an early hot spot for organized basketball. Pro teams such as the American Gears, Stags, Packers, and Zephyrs were all based in Chicago throughout the late 1940s and early 1950s. It wasn't until 1966 that the Bulls were established in the NBA. The franchise became a force to be reckoned with after it drafted Michael Jordan in 1984. Jordan would go on to lead the Bulls to six titles.

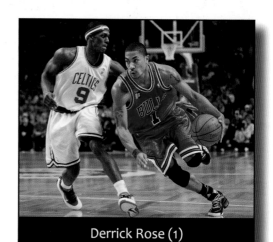
Derrick Rose (1)

Legends & Stars

Scottie Pippen (33)

Artis Gilmore	C	1976–1982	"A-Train" was a scoring, rebounding, and shot-blocking machine
Michael Jordan	G/F	1984–1993, 1995–1998	Widely considered the best player of all time, "Air" Jordan was a slam-dunking, tongue-wagging, trophy-winning legend
Bob Love	F	1969–1976	The smooth forward averaged 20-plus points per game in all but one of his Bulls seasons
Scottie Pippen	G/F	1987–1998, 2004	Michael Jordan's right-hand man played an important role in all six NBA titles with his superior ability to defend
Derrick Rose	G	2008–present	The 2008–2009 NBA Rookie of the Year was selected to the 2010 All-Star game
Jerry Sloan	G/F	1966–1976	Sloan rebounded extremely well for a guard and likely led the league in floor burns

By the Numbers

POINTS	Michael Jordan 1984–1993, 1995–1998 29,277	**STEALS**	Michael Jordan 2,306	
REBOUNDS	Michael Jordan 5,836	**BLOCKS**	Artis Gilmore 1976–1982 1,029	
ASSISTS	Michael Jordan 5,012	**THREES**	Kirk Hinrich 2003–present 812	

A Baseball Break

In the summer of 1994, 31-year-old Michael Jordan honed his baseball skills as a tall, athletic outfielder in the Chicago White Sox farm system. Having recently retired from the Bulls, he wanted a career change following the 1993 death of his father. Baseball was the answer. Though he had trouble hitting (.202 batting average), Jordan's baseball coaches hailed him for his tireless work ethic on the diamond. But the game of basketball came calling once again. Jordan went back to the Bulls in 1995, and the team won three more titles.

United Center

Change of Venue

Chicago Stadium was one of the loudest basketball arenas in the league from 1967 to 1994 when the Bulls played there. The stadium hosted the Bulls as they won their first three championships in 1991, 1992, and 1993. But in the 1994–1995 season, the Bulls moved into the United Center—where they soon won another three titles.

CLEVELAND CAVALIERS

First Season: 1970–1971

Franchise Record: 1,521–1,727

Home Arena: Quicken Loans Arena
(20,562 capacity) in Cleveland, Ohio

CHAMPIONSHIPS
None

The Cavaliers joined the NBA as an expansion team in 1970. The team enjoyed early success, nearly making the NBA Finals in 1976 before falling to Boston in the Eastern Conference Finals. The Cavs were frequently foiled by Michael Jordan's Chicago Bulls in the 1990s. But in 2003 Cleveland drafted local hero LeBron James from Akron, Ohio. The Cavs have been one of the NBA's most competitive teams since.

Daniel Gibson (1), 2007 Finals

Legends & Stars

Zydrunas Ilgauskas (11)

Austin Carr	G/F	1971–1980	In his first three seasons with the Cavs, Carr averaged more than 20 points per game
Brad Daugherty	C	1986–1994	Daugherty manned the middle for eight seasons before back injuries shortened his career
Zydrunas Ilgauskas	C	1997–present	The 7-foot 3-inch (221-centimeter) center is a two-time All-Star
LeBron James	G/F	2003–present	"King James" has won the league's MVP award and led his team to the NBA Finals
Mark Price	G	1986–1995	An excellent point guard with a knack for free throws and three-pointers, Price made four All-Star teams
Bingo Smith	G	1970–1979	When Smith would hit a three-pointer during a home game, the court announcer would yell "BINGO!"

By the Numbers

POINTS
LeBron James
2003–present
15,251

STEALS
LeBron James
955 →

REBOUNDS
Zydrunas Ilgauskas
1997–present
5,904

BLOCKS
Zydrunas Ilgauskas
1,269

ASSISTS
Mark Price
1986–1995
4,206

THREES
Mark Price
802

Dynamic Draft of '86

In 1986 the Cavaliers, coming off a season they finished 29–53, needed to give their roster a boost. The boost arrived with the NBA draft. The Cavs selected center Brad Daugherty, guard Ron Harper, and forward John "Hot Rod" Williams. They also received guard Mark Price from the Dallas Mavericks. All but Price made the 1986–1987 NBA All-Rookie Team, though Price would soon become an All-Star, and the Cavs were on their way up.

Brad Daugherty

Miracle of Richfield

In the 1975–1976 season, the Cavs made the playoffs for the first time in franchise history and became known as the Miracle of Richfield. In winning the playoff series against the Washington Bullets 4–3, the Cavs thrilled their fans with two one-point wins and a two-point win in the series finale at the Richfield Coliseum in Cleveland.

DALLAS MAVERICKS

First Season: 1980–1981

Franchise Record: 1,207–1,221
Home Arena: American Airlines Center (19,200 capacity) in Dallas, Texas

CHAMPIONSHIPS
None

Established in 1980 as an NBA expansion team, the Mavericks have become one of the NBA's most competitive franchises. The team's best season to date came in 2005–2006 when forward Dirk Nowitzki led his team to the NBA Finals. There the Mavs were beaten by the Miami Heat for the championship.

Jason Terry (31) shoots a three-pointer during the 2007 Finals.

Legends & Stars

Michael Finley (4)

Mark Aguirre	G/F	1981–1989	The three-time All-Star could score inside or out
Rolando Blackman	G/F	1981–1992	"Ro" was the second-leading scorer in Mavs history
Brad Davis	G	1980–1992	The first Maverick to have his number (15) retired
Michael Finley	G/F	1996–2005	Finley was a threat to drive to the hoop or elevate over the defense for a jumper
Dirk Nowitzki	F	1998–present	In 2007 the seven-footer with a three-point shooting touch became the first European player to win the league MVP

By the Numbers

POINTS	**Dirk Nowitzki** 1998–present 21,111	**STEALS**	**Derek Harper** 1,551	
REBOUNDS	**Dirk Nowitzki** 7,802	**BLOCKS**	**Shawn Bradley** 1997–2005 1,250	
ASSISTS	**Derek Harper** 1983–1994, 1996–1997 5,111	**THREES**	**Dirk Nowitzki** 1,131	

Texas Twist

Receiving league approval to bring an NBA franchise to Dallas in 1980, owners Norm Sonju and Don Carter needed a team name. They set up a contest for people to submit ideas, stating the new Dallas team needed something that represented Texas. They finally settled on Mavericks, possibly in part because a minority owner, actor James Garner, had starred in the popular TV western-comedy series, *Maverick*.

Mark Cuban

Intense Owner

Mark Cuban isn't your typical sports franchise owner. Often sitting near the end of the bench in casual clothes during games and badgering the officials, the dot-com multimillionaire fully supports his team. He has been fined by the league office for more money than any owner in NBA history—once $250,000 for misconduct during the 2006 NBA Finals.

DENVER NUGGETS

First Season: 1967–1968

Franchise Record: 1,732–1,768

Home Arena: Pepsi Center
(19,309 capacity) in Denver, Colorado

CHAMPIONSHIPS
None

Denver hosted an NBA franchise named the Nuggets for the 1949–1950 season, but the team quickly folded. Seventeen years later the city was awarded another pro team. The Denver Rockets began play in the American Basketball Association in 1967. They were renamed the Nuggets in 1974 and played in the ABA's last Finals in 1976, losing to the New York Nets. The next season the Nuggets and star guard David Thompson moved to the NBA. Today forward Carmelo Anthony leads the way in Denver.

Carmelo Anthony (15)

Legends & Stars

Dan Issel (44)

Carmelo Anthony	F	2003–present	"Melo" is able to score with ease; the small forward stepped up his defense after playing on the 2008 U.S. Olympic team
Byron Beck	F/C	1967–1977	The first Denver player to have his number (40) retired
Alex English	F	1979–1990	"The Blade" was the Nuggets' all-time leading scorer; the team retired his number 2 jersey
Dan Issel	F/C	1975–1985	"The Horse" was named ABA Rookie of the Year in 1970–1971
Lafayette Lever	G	1984–1990	The shifty guard was small, but "Fat" could nail three-pointers, dish out assists, and play tight defense
David Thompson	G/F	1975–1982	"Skywalker" had an amazing 44- to 48-inch (112- to 122-cm) vertical leap and used it to throw down slam dunks

By the Numbers

POINTS	**Alex English** 1979–1990 21,645	
STEALS	**Lafayette Lever** 1984–1990 1,167	
REBOUNDS	**Dan Issel** 1975–1985 6,630	
BLOCKS	**Dikembe Mutombo** 1991–1996 1,486	
ASSISTS	**Alex English** 3,679	
THREES	**J.R. Smith** 2006–present 644	

Fashionably Unfashionable

Though they're now considered retro fashionable, the Nuggets' uniforms in the 1980s were hard on the eyes. The jersey front's logo had purple, blue, red, orange, green, and yellow rectangles arranged in a Rocky Mountains design. The Nuggets coach in those years, Doug Moe, was well known for his sloppy way of dressing. "I've never been comfortable with a tie," said Moe at one point. "In my mind, ties are ridiculous for a coach to wear. This is an emotional business."

George Karl

Courageous Coach

Entering his sixth season as the Nuggets' coach, George Karl was diagnosed with throat cancer midway through the 2009–2010 season. He continued to coach his team between radiation treatments. Denver ended the season with a 53–29 record and tied Utah for the best record in the Northwest Division in the Western Conference.

DETROIT PISTONS

First Season: 1948–1949

Franchise Record: 2,427–2,465

Home Arena: The Palace of Auburn Hills
(22,076 capacity) in Auburn Hills, Michigan

CHAMPIONSHIPS
1989, 1990, 2004

The Fort Wayne Zollner Pistons began play in the old National Basketball League in 1941. They were named after their owner, Fred Zollner, a businessman in the Detroit automobile and piston industry. In 1948 the Pistons dropped "Zollner" from their name and joined the Basketball Association of America. The next year the NBL and BAA merged to become the NBA. The Pistons, who moved to Detroit in 1957, enjoyed their best seasons in 1988–1989 and 1989–1990 when they won back-to-back NBA titles.

Chauncey Billups, 2004 Finals

Legends & Stars

Isiah Thomas (11)

Joe Dumars	G	1985–1999	A defensive genius who could consistently guard Michael Jordan; Dumars is now in Pistons' management
Richard Hamilton	G/F	2002–present	"Rip" often weaves around screens to receive the ball for his signature jump shot
Bill Laimbeer	F	1982–1994	A member of Detroit's championship teams, Laimbeer was an accurate shooter and hard-working rebounder
Bob Lanier	C	1970–1980	Lanier was an eight-time All-Star for the Pistons
Tayshaun Prince	F	2002–present	Despite a slim build, Prince excels on the defensive end
Isiah Thomas	G	1981–1994	Thomas was one of the premier point guards of the 1980s
Ben Wallace	F/C	2000–2006, 2009–present	The leading shot-blocker in Pistons history was a spark behind Detroit's defensive-minded, 2004 championship team

By the Numbers

POINTS	**Isiah Thomas** 1981–1994 18,822	**STEALS**	**Isiah Thomas** 1,861
REBOUNDS	**Bill Laimbeer** 1982–1994 9,430	**BLOCKS**	**Ben Wallace** 2000–2006, 2009–present 1,381
ASSISTS	**Isiah Thomas** 9,061	**THREES**	**Joe Dumars** 1985–1999 990 ⟶

Most Points Ever

Fans at the December 13, 1983, game got their money's worth. The Denver Nuggets, one of the NBA's highest-scoring teams in the '80s, went on a scoring frenzy with the Pistons. Both teams sprinted up and down the court to the NBA's highest point total ever. When the smoke cleared, the Pistons had won 186-184 in triple overtime. Isiah Thomas scored 47 points, and John Lang and Kelly Tripucka chipped in 41 and 35 points.

Bill Laimbeer (40) and Dennis Rodman (10)

Bad Boys

The Pistons' back-to-back NBA championships in 1989 and 1990 were won with great guard play, fantastic coaching, and a bullying nature. With such players as Rick Mahorn, Bill Laimbeer, and Dennis Rodman, the Pistons were nicknamed the "Bad Boys." They were just as likely to out-elbow, out-trash talk, and out-clobber their opponents as to outscore them.

21

GOLDEN STATE WARRIORS

First Season: 1946–1947

Franchise Record: 2,293–2,705
Home Arena: Oracle Arena
(19,596 capacity) in Oakland, California

CHAMPIONSHIPS
1946 (BAA), 1956, 1975

The Warriors began play in Philadelphia in the Basketball Association of America in 1946. They won the BAA title their first year, and followed it with an NBA title in 1956. In the 1960s the Warriors were led by the stellar play of legendary center Wilt Chamberlain, who was with the team when it moved from Philly to San Francisco in 1962. The team changed its name to the Golden State Warriors in 1971, and in 1975 the Warriors won their third title.

Stephen Curry

Legends & Stars

Monta Ellis

Paul Arizin	G	1950–1962	The 10-time All-Star was elected to the Hall of Fame
Rick Barry	F	1965–1967, 1972–1978	Famous for his underhand free-throw shooting, Barry was the Finals MVP in 1975
Wilt Chamberlain	C	1959–1968	"The Stilt" was the leading scorer in Warriors' franchise history and went to the All-Star Game 13 times
Stephen Curry	G	2009–present	The Warriors' rising star has the ability to shoot from anywhere on the court
Monta Ellis	G	2005–present	Ellis averaged 25.5 points per game in the 2009–2010 season
Chris Mullin	G	1985–1997, 2000–2001	Five-time All-Star had one of the smoothest shots in the game
Nate Thurmond	F/C	1963–1974	A master of the blocked shot, Thurmond was a fan favorite for his work around the boards and his clutch performances

By the Numbers

POINTS
Wilt Chamberlain
1959–1968
17,783

STEALS
Chris Mullin
1985–1997, 2000–2001
1,360

REBOUNDS
Nate Thurmond
1963–1974
12,771

BLOCKS
Adonal Foyle
1997–2007
1,140

ASSISTS
Guy Rodgers
1958–1966
4,855

THREES
Jason Richardson
2001–2007
700

Wilt's 100-Pointer

Scoring in double digits is one thing for an individual player, but triple digits? Wilt Chamberlain became the only player to accomplish the feat. On March 2, 1962, he scored exactly 100 points in a 169-147 win over the New York Knickerbockers. Chamberlain made 36 of 63 field goals and 28 of 32 free throws.

Wilt Chamberlain (13)

Golden Handle

The Warriors made history when they changed their name from the San Francisco Warriors to the Golden State Warriors in 1971. They became the only NBA team without a state or city as part of their official team name.

HOUSTON ROCKETS

First Season: 1967–1968

Franchise Record: 1,779–1,715
Home Arena: Toyota Center
(18,300 capacity) in Houston, Texas

CHAMPIONSHIPS
1994, 1995

The Rockets joined the NBA as an expansion team in 1967 and played their first four seasons in sunny San Diego. The team did not have a great deal of success there and made the move to Houston in 1971. Once in Houston the Rockets made steady progress, finishing runners-up in 1981 and 1986 before taking home back-to-back championships in 1994 and 1995. Rockets fans remember those championship teams for their big hearts and the smooth play of center Hakeem Olajuwon.

Yao Ming (11)

Legends & Stars

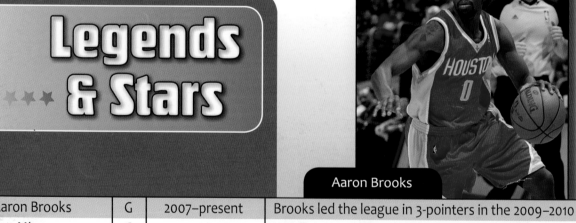
Aaron Brooks

Aaron Brooks	G	2007–present	Brooks led the league in 3-pointers in the 2009–2010 season
Yao Ming	C	2002–present	Yao dominates the court with his unique blend of size (7 feet 6 inches; 229 centimeters) and shooting touch
Calvin Murphy	G	1971–1983	The Hall of Fame guard was a threat at the free-throw line
Hakeem Olajuwon	C	1984–2001	"The Dream" achieved 12 All-Star selections, two Defensive Player of the Year awards, one MVP, and two NBA titles
Rudy Tomjanovich	F	1971–1981	"Rudy T" averaged more than 18 points per game with the Rockets; he also coached Houston to two NBA titles

By the Numbers

POINTS	Hakeem Olajuwon 1984–2001 26,511	**STEALS**	Hakeem Olajuwon 2,088	
REBOUNDS	Hakeem Olajuwon 13,382	**BLOCKS**	Hakeem Olajuwon 3,740	
ASSISTS	Calvin Murphy 1971–1983 4,402	**THREES**	Vernon Maxwell 1990–1995 730	

Prepared for Liftoff

When the San Diego Rockets moved to Houston, their name was perfect. It fit well since the NASA space program is located in Houston.

Native Son

Clyde Drexler and his University of Houston Cougars teammates (including Hakeem Olajuwon) made an impression on college basketball fans with their slam-dunking ways in the early 1980s. They called themselves "Phi Slama Jama" and finished runner-up twice in NCAA championship games. Houston basketball fans sadly said goodbye to Drexler when he was drafted by the Portland Trail Blazers. But in 1995 the Rockets made a trade that reunited Drexler with Olajuwon and the city of Houston. The result was an NBA championship trophy.

Clyde Drexler (22)

INDIANA PACERS

First Season: 1967–1968

Franchise Record: 1,766–1,734

Home Arena: Conseco Fieldhouse
(18,345 capacity) in Indianapolis, Indiana

CHAMPIONSHIPS
1970 (ABA), 1972 (ABA), 1973 (ABA)

The Pacers started out in the American Basketball Association in 1967 and won three championships in the league's nine-year existence. In 1976 the Pacers made the move to the NBA along with the Denver Nuggets, the New York Nets, and the San Antonio Spurs. Long-range bomber Reggie Miller and coach Larry Bird led the Pacers to the 2000 NBA Finals, where they lost a hard-fought series to the Los Angeles Lakers.

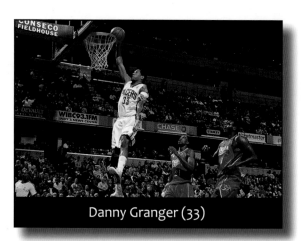
Danny Granger (33)

Rik Smits (45)

Danny Granger	F	2005–present	Granger was named the NBA's Most Improved Player in 2009
Mark Jackson	G	1994–2000	Jackson's passing skills led the Pacers to the 2000 NBA Finals
George McGinnis	F	1971–1975, 1980–1982	Holds the Pacers' single-game records for points (58) and rebounds (37); won the ABA's MVP in 1974–1975
Reggie Miller	G	1987–2005	The five-time All-Star was a pure shooter from three-point land
Rik Smits	C	1988–2000	The "Dunkin' Dutchman" had the shooting touch of guards half his size

By the Numbers

POINTS	**Reggie Miller** 1987–2005 25,279	
REBOUNDS	**Mel Daniels** 1968–1974 7,643	
ASSISTS	**Reggie Miller** 4,141	
STEALS	**Reggie Miller** 1,505 ⟶	
BLOCKS	**Jermaine O'Neal** 2000–2008 1,245	
THREES	**Reggie Miller** 2,560	

8 Points in 8.9 Seconds

With less than 20 seconds left in Game 1 of the Eastern Conference Finals on May 7, 1995, the Knicks were leading the Pacers 105-99. Then the Pacers' Reggie Miller went wild. With 16.4 seconds left, he hit a three-pointer. Then he stole the in-bounds pass from the Knicks and stepped back to hit another three. With the game tied, John Starks of the Knicks missed a pair of free throws. Miller snared the rebound, was fouled, and with 7.5 seconds left, made both free throws. The Pacers won the game and the series.

"Larry Legend" as Coach

In 1997 Indiana native and NBA superstar Larry Bird became head coach of the Indiana Pacers. Despite having no background in coaching, the former Indiana State hoops star led the Pacers to a 58–24 record and was named NBA Coach of the Year. His team made it to Game 7 in the Eastern Conference Finals but lost to the Chicago Bulls. In 2000 Bird led the Pacers to the NBA finals, where they lost to the Los Angeles Lakers. Bird retired from coaching after the 1999–2000 season, but he rejoined the Pacers in 2003 as president of basketball operations.

Larry Bird

LOS ANGELES CLIPPERS

Franchise Record: 1,175–2,073
Home Arena: Staples Center
(18,997 capacity) in Los Angeles, California

CHAMPIONSHIPS
None

First Season: 1970–1971

Chris Kaman (35)

In 1970 the Buffalo Braves joined the NBA as an expansion team. They lasted eight seasons in Buffalo, New York, before moving to San Diego to become the Clippers. There they took a big chance on trading for promising young center Bill Walton, but Walton's health caused him to miss large chunks of playing time. The franchise eventually packed up and moved to Los Angeles in 1984. There the Clippers have found limited success, posting just two winning seasons in their first 25 seasons in L.A.

Legends & Stars

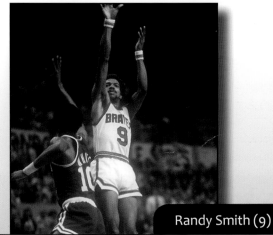
Randy Smith (9)

Eric Gordon	G	2008–present	As a rookie, Gordon scored 41 points in a single game
Chris Kaman	C	2003–present	Kaman's inside game and rebounding skills make him a threat in the post
Danny Manning	F	1988–1994	After winning an NCAA title at Kansas, Manning was the No. 1 overall pick in the 1988 NBA draft
Bob McAdoo	F	1972–1976	The 1975 NBA MVP led the league in scoring three times for the Buffalo Braves
Randy Smith	G	1971–1979, 1982–1983	The MVP of the 1978 All-Star Game holds the franchise record for points, assists, and steals

By the Numbers

POINTS	Randy Smith 1971–1979, 1982–1983 12,735	**STEALS**	Randy Smith 1,072	
REBOUNDS	Elton Brand 2001–2008 4,710	**BLOCKS**	Benoit Benjamin 1985–1991 1,117	
ASSISTS	Randy Smith 3,498	**THREES**	Eric Piatkowski 1994–2003 738	

Time Share

The Clippers and the Lakers, both located in Los Angeles, share the Staples Center, a multipurpose arena that opened in 1999. Each team has its own floor. The Clippers play on a red, white, and blue floor, and the Lakers play on a purple and gold floor.

Clipper Curse

The Clippers have only made the playoffs seven times in their first 40 seasons. Looking to turn things around with the No. 1 draft pick in 2009, Los Angeles selected University of Oklahoma star Blake Griffin. Unfortunately, Griffin sustained a season-ending injury to his knee before playing a single regular-season game. Many of the Clippers' past picks have also had serious injuries.

Blake Griffin

29

LOS ANGELES LAKERS

First Season: 1948–1949

The Lakers were aptly named when they started in Minnesota, the Land of 10,000 Lakes. There the Minneapolis Lakers won five championships behind the talents of George Mikan, the first great pro center in organized basketball. In 1960 the Lakers moved west to Los Angeles. The team has hosted many NBA greats who helped the Lakers to NBA titles.

Franchise Record: 3,027–1,866

Home Arena: Staples Center (18,997 capacity) in Los Angeles, California

CHAMPIONSHIPS

1949 (BAA), 1950, 1952, 1953, 1954, 1972, 1980, 1982, 1985, 1987, 1988, 2000, 2001, 2002, 2009

2009 NBA champions

Legends & Stars

Kobe Bryant (24)

Kareem Abdul-Jabbar	C	1975–1989	Abdul-Jabbar scored 38,387 career points, the most in NBA history; he was inducted into the Hall of Fame in 1995
Elgin Baylor	F	1958–1972	Baylor pounded the glass and lit up the scoreboard on his way to 11 All-Star games
Kobe Bryant	G	1996–present	Bryant directed the Lakers to four championship titles and led the NBA in scoring four times
Earvin Johnson	G	1979–1991, 1995–1996	"Magic" led the Lakers to five titles in the 1980s and won the league's MVP in 1987, 1989, and 1990
George Mikan	F/C	1948–1956	Basketball's first dominant big man led the Minneapolis Lakers to five titles
Jerry West	G	1960–1974	West was the main scorer for the Lakers throughout the 1960s and into the 1970s

By the Numbers

POINTS
Kobe Bryant
1996–present
25,790

REBOUNDS
Elgin Baylor
1958–1972
11,463

ASSISTS
Earvin Johnson
1979–1991, 1995–1996
10,141

STEALS
Earvin Johnson
1,724

BLOCKS
Kareem Abdul-Jabbar
1975–1989
2,694

THREES
Kobe Bryant
1,303

Centers of Attention

From Wilt Chamberlain and Kareem Abdul-Jabbar to Shaquille O'Neal, the Lakers have had tremendous talent under the hoop. The Lakers latest big man, center Andrew Bynum, is following in their footsteps and becoming a threat in the post.

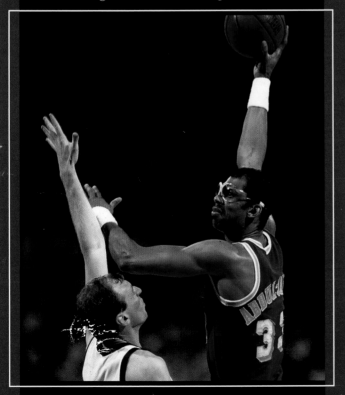

Kareem Abdul-Jabbar (33)

Showtime

The 1980s featured one of the most exciting teams in NBA history: the Lakers' "Showtime." Kareem Abdul-Jabbar, A.C. Green, and Kurt Rambis were key rebounders, and they would throw quick outlet passes to point guard Magic Johnson. Magic would race down court with players such as Michael Cooper, Byron Scott, or James Worthy filling the lane and swooping in for the slam. The quick-moving Lakers teams brought home five titles in the 1980s.

MEMPHIS GRIZZLIES

Franchise Record: 404–794
Home Arena: FedEx Forum
(18,165 capacity) in Memphis, Tennessee

CHAMPIONSHIPS
None

First Season: 1995–1996

The Grizzlies were born in 1995 in Vancouver, Canada, via NBA expansion with another Canadian franchise, the Toronto Raptors. They didn't break the .500 mark in wins for six seasons in Vancouver. Management looked to turn things around when they moved the team to Memphis in 2001. In the Grizzlies' third season in their new city, they finally made the playoffs. They returned to the playoffs in 2005 and 2006 as well.

O.J. Mayo at the 2009 Rookie Challenge

Legends & Stars

Rudy Gay (22)

Shareef Abdur-Rahim	G/F	1996–2001	Abdur-Rahim constantly put up double-doubles in points and rebounds
Pau Gasol	F	2001–2008	Gasol won the 2001–2002 Rookie of the Year award for his scoring and rebounding skills
Rudy Gay	F	2006–present	Gay's ability to cut to the basket goes well with a sweet stroke from the perimeter
O.J. Mayo	G	2008–present	Rising star has a shooter's touch and great ball control
Bryant Reeves	C	1995–2001	"Big Country" was the Grizzlies' first-ever draft pick in 1995
Lorenzen Wright	F	2001–2006	A hometown favorite from Memphis, Wright was a fighter in the post

By the Numbers

POINTS	**Pau Gasol** 2001–2008 8,966	**STEALS**	**Shane Battier** 2001–2006 507	
REBOUNDS	**Pau Gasol** 4,096	**BLOCKS**	**Pau Gasol** 877	
ASSISTS	**Jason Williams** 2001–2005 2,041	**THREES**	**Mike Miller** 2003–2008 737	

Into the Playoffs

Through their first six seasons, the Grizzlies failed to reach even 25 wins, much less make the playoffs. But in their seventh season, the team moved to Memphis, and in their eighth season, veteran coach Hubie Brown took over after a miserable start. Finally, in their ninth season, the Grizzlies recorded their first winning regular season (50–32) and made the playoffs. The playoff appearance didn't last long, though; the Grizzlies fell to the San Antonio Spurs in the first round in four games.

Going with Grizzlies

If grizzly bears don't live as far south as Memphis, Tennessee, how did the team get its name? The franchise got its start in Vancouver, British Columbia, Canada, a place well-known for its grizzly bears. Franchise owners almost named the team the Mounties after Canada's famous Royal Canadian Mounted Police, but Grizzlies ended up being the choice. Once the team moved to Memphis in 2001, team officials found that the fans preferred to keep the name.

The Grizzlies' mascot, Grizz

MIAMI HEAT

First Season: 1988–1989

Franchise Record: 861–911

Home Arena: American Airlines Arena (19,600 capacity) in Miami, Florida

CHAMPIONSHIP
2006

Michael Beasley (30)

The Heat was a 1988 expansion team that started hot right from the start. In just its fourth season, the team made the playoffs. By the late 1990s, coach Pat Riley had transformed the Heat into a true contender. In 2006 guard Dwyane Wade and center Shaquille O'Neal led Miami to the NBA title.

Legends & Stars

Alonzo Mourning (33)

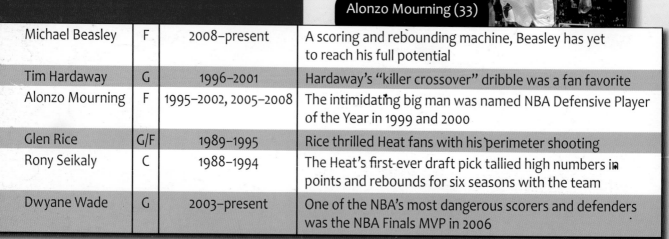

Michael Beasley	F	2008–present	A scoring and rebounding machine, Beasley has yet to reach his full potential
Tim Hardaway	G	1996–2001	Hardaway's "killer crossover" dribble was a fan favorite
Alonzo Mourning	F	1995–2002, 2005–2008	The intimidating big man was named NBA Defensive Player of the Year in 1999 and 2000
Glen Rice	G/F	1989–1995	Rice thrilled Heat fans with his perimeter shooting
Rony Seikaly	C	1988–1994	The Heat's first-ever draft pick tallied high numbers in points and rebounds for six seasons with the team
Dwyane Wade	G	2003–present	One of the NBA's most dangerous scorers and defenders was the NBA Finals MVP in 2006

By the Numbers

POINTS	**Dwyane Wade** 2003–present 11,967	
REBOUNDS	**Alonzo Mourning** 1995–2002, 2005–2008 4,807	
ASSISTS	**Dwyane Wade** 3,126	
STEALS	**Dwyane Wade** 862	→
BLOCKS	**Alonzo Mourning** 1,625	
THREES	**Tim Hardaway** 1996–2001 806	

Heating Up

When it came time to name a pro basketball team in Miami, a contest was held. Some of the names suggested were Sharks, Barracudas, Flamingos, Palm Trees, Beaches, Heat, Suntan, Shade, Tornadoes, and Floridians. Team owners picked Heat, one of only four NBA names not ending in s.

Big Man in the Middle

At 7 feet 2 inches (188 centimeters) and nearly 250 pounds (113 kilograms), Shaquille O'Neal was a dominant force on the basketball court. Teamed with talented young guard Dwyane Wade, O'Neal helped the Heat to the 2006 NBA title. Though he was traded to Phoenix just two seasons later, he is still beloved by Miami fans.

Dwyane Wade (left) and Shaquille O'Neal

MILWAUKEE BUCKS

Franchise Record: 1,790–1,622
Home Arena: Bradley Center
(18,717 capacity) in Milwaukee, Wisconsin

CHAMPIONSHIP
1971

First Season: 1968–1969

The Bucks began play in the NBA in 1968 as an expansion team. In their second year they drafted center Kareem Abdul-Jabbar, and the wins started piling up. In the team's third season, Abdul-Jabbar teamed with veteran Oscar Robertson to lead the Bucks to the 1970–1971 NBA title. The Bucks featured strong teams throughout the 1980s. They also nearly made the NBA Finals in 2001, but they lost to the Philadelphia 76ers in the Eastern Conference Finals

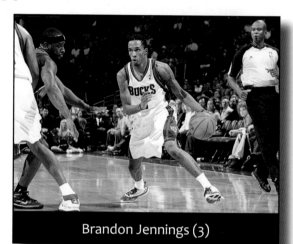

Brandon Jennings (3)

Legends & Stars

Andrew Bogut (6)

Kareem Abdul-Jabbar	C	1969–1975	Abdul-Jabbar picked up three league MVPs and a championship title in his six seasons with the Bucks
Andrew Bogut	C	2005–present	The Australian center combines great passing and shooting skills with all-around smart play
Bob Dandridge	F	1969–1977	The four-time All-Star was a key member of the 1971 Bucks
Sidney Moncrief	G	1979–1989	"Super Sid" was a high-rising marvel with a smooth jumper and a knack for coming through in the clutch
Oscar Robertson	G	1970–1974	Though he arrived in Milwaukee at the end of his career, "The Big O" was a key part of Milwaukee's championship team
Glenn Robinson	F	1994–2002	"Big Dog" was a pure scorer with quick baseline moves and an accurate mid-range jump shot

By the Numbers

POINTS	**Kareem Abdul-Jabbar** 1969–1975 14,211	**STEALS** **Quinn Buckner** 1976–1982 1,042
REBOUNDS	**Kareem Abdul-Jabbar** 7,161	**BLOCKS** **Alton Listner** 1981–1986, 1995 804
ASSISTS	**Paul Pressey** 1982–1990 3,272	**THREES** **Ray Allen** 1996–2003 1,051

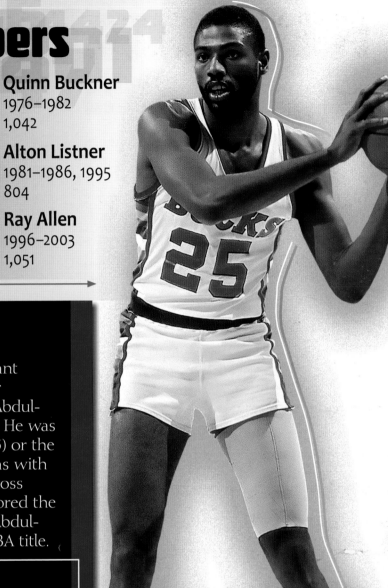

Lucky Flip

In the summer of 1969, dominant center Lew Alcindor—who later changed his name to Kareem Abdul-Jabbar—entered the NBA draft. He was going to either the Bucks (27–55) or the Phoenix Suns (16–66), the teams with the worst two records. A coin toss decided the outcome. Luck favored the Bucks, and two seasons later, Abdul-Jabbar led Milwaukee to the NBA title.

Kareem Abdul-Jabbar (33)

Un-tame Nickname

One of the most unique nicknames in the NBA belongs to Milwaukee. "Bucks" was chosen in a 1968 naming contest in which more than 14,000 fans gave their suggestions. Other suggestions included Skunks, Beavers, Stags, Hornets, Stallions, Ponies, and Badgers.

37

MINNESOTA TIMBERWOLVES

First Season: 1989–1990

Franchise Record: 688–1,002
Home Arena: Target Center (20,500 capacity) in Minneapolis, Minnesota

CHAMPIONSHIPS
None

When the NBA added two teams in 1989, the Timberwolves were born. Minnesota basketball fans had enjoyed the fine play of the Minneapolis Lakers from 1947 to 1960 before the team moved to Los Angeles. In 2004 the Wolves had the best record in the NBA, making it to the playoffs for the eighth straight time. After winning the first two series, Minnesota lost steam in the Western Conference Finals, losing 4–2 to the Los Angeles Lakers.

Kevin Love (42)

Legends & Stars

Wally Szczerbiak (10)

Kevin Garnett	F	1995–2007	Drafted out of high school in 1995, "Da Kid" won the NBA MVP in 2003–2004
Tom Gugliotta	F	1995–1998	"Googs" was an All-Star in 1997 and could play in the post or out on the wings
Kevin Love	F	2008–present	Love is a rebounding machine who starred at UCLA
Sam Mitchell	F	1989–1992, 1995–2002	One of the original Timberwolves, Mitchell was a reliable forward during his two stints in Minnesota
Wally Szczerbiak	G	1999–2005	Szczerbiak could drive to the hoop or hit three-pointers

By the Numbers

POINTS	Kevin Garnett 1995–2007 19,041	**STEALS**	Kevin Garnett 1,282
REBOUNDS	Kevin Garnett 10,542	**BLOCKS**	Kevin Garnett 1,576
ASSISTS	Kevin Garnett 4,146	**THREES**	Anthony Peeler 1998–2003 465

Somber Legacy

The Timberwolves' first and only retirement of one of their players' numbers came in 2000. That year the team raised Malik Sealy's number 2 to the rafters of Target Center. Sealy, a popular player whose career had been revived in Minnesota, was killed in a car accident following a birthday celebration for teammate and friend Kevin Garnett. The driver of the other vehicle was going the wrong way on the highway.

The Franchise

Hopes were high when the Wolves drafted Kevin Garnett out of high school in 1995. Paired with Stephon Marbury in 1996, KG led Minnesota to a 40–42 record and their first playoff appearance. Although the Wolves made the playoffs for eight consecutive seasons behind "The Franchise," they never made it to the NBA Finals. After 12 seasons in Minnesota, he was traded to the Boston Celtics in 2007.

Kevin Garnett (21), 2004 playoffs

39

NEW JERSEY NETS

First Season: 1967–1968

Franchise Record: 1,536–1,964
Home Arena: Citi Arena
(19,990 capacity) in East Rutherford, New Jersey

CHAMPIONSHIPS
1974 (ABA), 1976 (ABA)

The New Jersey Americans began play in the ABA in 1967. The next season they packed up and headed to New York as the Nets. They won two ABA championships behind the play of Julius "Dr. J." Erving before moving to the NBA in 1976. In 1977 the Nets moved back to New Jersey, where they reached the NBA Finals in 2002 and 2003 behind point guard Jason Kidd.

The Nets' mascot, Sly the Silver Fox

Devin Harris (34)

Derrick Coleman	F	1990–1995	Coleman scared away opponents with his growl and jumper
Darryl Dawkins	C	1982–1987	Dawkins shattered backboards with spine-shaking dunks and set the NBA season record for most fouls (386) in 1984
Devin Harris	G	2008–present	Harris figures to thrill Nets fans for years to come with his lightning-fast pull-up jumpers, quick passes, and steady defense
Jason Kidd	G	2001–2008	Kidd was a triple-double threat who could thread passes through defenders with ease
Buck Williams	F/C	1981–1989	Williams was a tough rebounder and defender in the paint for eight seasons with the Nets

By the Numbers

POINTS	**Buck Williams** 1981–1989 10,440	**STEALS**	**Jason Kidd** 950	
REBOUNDS	**Buck Williams** 7,576	**BLOCKS**	**George Johnson** 1977–1980, 1984–1985 863	
ASSISTS	**Jason Kidd** 2001–2008 4,620	**THREES**	**Jason Kidd** 813	

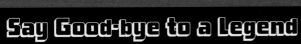

What a Kidd

Coming off a 26–52 record in 2000–2001, the Nets needed to try something new. They traded Stephon Marbury and Johnny Newman to the Phoenix Suns for Jason Kidd. The point guard immediately helped the Nets to an amazing turnaround. He led New Jersey all the way to the NBA Finals, where they were bested by the Los Angeles Lakers. The next season, Kidd again helped the Nets to the Finals, but they lost to the San Antonio Spurs in six games.

Say Good-bye to a Legend

Julius Erving helped the Nets win ABA titles in 1974 and 1976 and was named league MVP in each of his first three seasons in a Nets uniform. It came as a shock when the Nets decided to trade him. The Nets were set to join the NBA in 1976 and move the franchise from New York to New Jersey. Money was tight, and Erving was hoping to renegotiate his contract. Owner Roy Boe worried that if he paid Erving more money, it would come at the expense of the franchise's survival in the new league. Boe sent Dr. J to the Philadelphia 76ers, and though the Nets survived, it was years before they found much success.

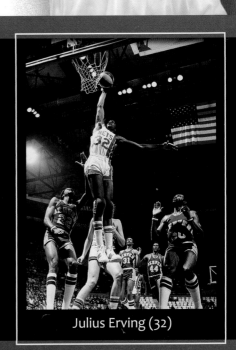

Julius Erving (32)

NEW ORLEANS HORNETS

First Season: 1988–1989

In 1988 the Charlotte Hornets opened play in the NBA as an expansion team. The Hornets' first star was rugged center Alonzo Mourning, who led the team to its first run at the playoffs in 1993. In 2002 the ballclub moved to New Orleans. Hurricane Katrina devastated the area in 2005, and the team played parts of two seasons in Oklahoma City before returning to New Orleans full-time in 2007.

Franchise Record: 867–905
Home Arena: New Orleans Arena
(18,000 capacity) in New Orleans, Louisiana

CHAMPIONSHIPS
None

Chris Paul (3)

Legends & Stars

David West (30)

Muggsy Bogues	G	1988–1997	The NBA's shortest player (5 feet 3 inches; 160 centimeters) excelled in the league because of his speed and quick hands
Dell Curry	G	1988–1998	One of the league's deadliest pure shooters in the 1990s became the franchise's all-time scoring leader
Larry Johnson	F	1991–1996	Two-time All-Star was the 1991 No. 1 overall pick in the draft
Alonzo Mourning	C	1992–1995	"Zo" averaged more than 20 points and 10 rebounds per game in three seasons as a Hornet
Chris Paul	G	2005–present	One of the quickest point guards in the game, Paul led the NBA in steals three times
David West	F	2003–present	West is a tough defender who can add up the points and crash the boards

By the Numbers

POINTS
Dell Curry
1988–1998
9,839

STEALS
Muggsy Bogues
1,067

REBOUNDS
P.J. Brown
2000–2006
4,203

BLOCKS
Alonzo Mourning
1992–1995
684

ASSISTS
Muggsy Bogues
1988–1997
5,557

THREES
Dell Curry
929

Star-Studded Return

In 2005 Hurricane Katrina devastated the city of New Orleans. Some people thought the team would stay in Oklahoma City—the city that hosted the Hornets while New Orleans was being rebuilt. But the Hornets returned to New Orleans for the 2007–2008 season ready to play. They hosted the All-Star game, posted their best season ever (56–26), and made the playoffs.

The Hornets' mascot, Super Hugo, performs an amazing dunk during a 2008 playoff game.

Historical Name

When owners of the new NBA basketball franchise in Charlotte called their team the Spirit, the name didn't go over so well. As a result, fans were allowed to vote on four nicknames: Gold, Knights, Spirit, and Hornets. The Hornets nickname came from the Revolutionary War. British General Charles Cornwallis wrote to England's King George III that battling in the Carolinas was like fighting in a hornet's nest.

NEW YORK KNICKS

First Season: 1946–1947

Franchise Record: 2,483–2,516
Home Arena: Madison Square Garden
(19,763 capacity) in New York, New York

CHAMPIONSHIPS
1970, 1973

The New York Knickerbockers started play in the Basketball Association of America in 1946. They were one of three BAA teams to survive after their move to the NBA. In the early 1970s, the Knicks played great defense that led to two NBA titles. In the 1980s and 1990s, center Patrick Ewing dominated the glass and the scoreboards.

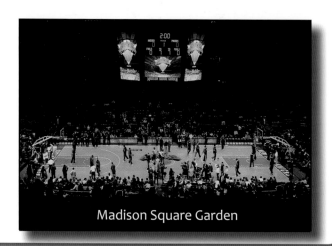
Madison Square Garden

Legends & Stars

Patrick Ewing (33)

Bill Bradley	G/F	1967–1977	"Dollar Bill" was a steady player for the Knicks; he became a U.S. senator after retiring from basketball
Patrick Ewing	C	1985–2000	The franchise leader in games played, points, rebounds, blocks, and steals was an 11-time All-Star
Walt Frazier	G	1967–1977	An amazing defender with quick hands, Frazier set the tone for the championship Knicks teams in the early 1970s
Danilo Gallinari	F	2008–present	Gallinari has become a threat from the perimeter, hitting 186 three-pointers in the 2009–2010 season
Earl Monroe	G	1971–1980	With a high-bouncing dribble and a knack for making hard plays look easy, "Earl the Pearl" was a four-time All-Star
Willis Reed	F	1964–1974	Reed was named MVP of the 1969–1970 season, All-Star game, and playoffs

By the Numbers

POINTS	**Patrick Ewing** 1985–2000 23,665	
REBOUNDS	**Patrick Ewing** 10,759	
ASSISTS	**Walt Frazier** 1967–1977 4,791	
STEALS	**Patrick Ewing** 1,061	
BLOCKS	**Patrick Ewing** 2,758	
THREES	**John Starks** 1990–1998 982 ⟶	

Literary Origins

The New York team went way back to get its name. In 1809 author Washington Irving—of *The Legend of Sleepy Hollow* fame—created a fictitious author/historian named Diedrich Knickerbocker. The name has since become a nickname for New Yorkers. The basketball team is more commonly known as the Knicks.

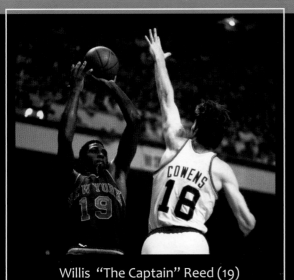

Willis "The Captain" Reed (19)

Nicknames for the Knicks

The Knicks championship teams in 1970 and 1973 had a host of players with fancy nicknames, including Walt "Clyde" Frazier, Dave "The Butcher" DeBusschere, Willis "The Captain" Reed, Dave "The Rave" Stallworth, "Dollar" Bill Bradley, Dick "Fall Back Baby" Barnett, Nate "The Snake" Bowman, Earl "The Pearl" Monroe, Phil "Action" Jackson, John "G-Man" Gianelli, Dean "The Dream" Meminger, and Harthorne "Wingy" Wingo. Even the coach, William "Red" Holzman, had a nickname.

OKLAHOMA CITY THUNDER

Franchise Record: 1,818–1,676
Home Arena: Ford Center
(19,599 capacity) in Oklahoma City, Oklahoma

CHAMPIONSHIP
1979

First Season: 1967–1968

The Seattle SuperSonics originated in 1967 as an NBA expansion team. One of the first big stars in Sonics' team history was the rim-rattling Spencer Haywood. In 1979 the Sonics brought home the franchise's only NBA title with a roster that thrilled Seattle fans with their team-oriented play. In 2008 the Sonics moved from Washington to Oklahoma City and were renamed the Thunder.

Russell Westbrook (0)

Legends & Stars

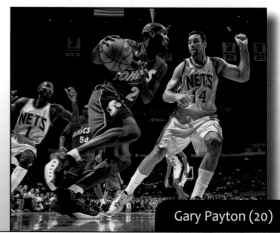
Gary Payton (20)

Freddie Brown	G	1971–1984	"Downtown" Freddie Brown was a lights-out shooter and a valuable sixth man for 13 seasons in Seattle
Kevin Durant	F	2007–present	The 2007–2008 Rookie of the Year has a unique blend of height (6 feet 10 inches; 208 centimeters) and shooting ability
Shawn Kemp	F	1989–1997	An impressive dunker and supreme athlete, Kemp was the Sonics' go-to big man for eight seasons
Gary Payton	G	1990–2003	"The Glove" smothered opposing guards with his tireless defense while putting up big numbers on offense
Jack Sikma	C	1977–1986	Seven-time All-Star averaged a double-double per game in nine seasons as a Sonic

By the Numbers

POINTS	**Gary Payton** 1990–2003 18,207	**STEALS**	**Gary Payton** 2,107	
REBOUNDS	**Jack Sikma** 1977–1986 7,729	**BLOCKS**	**Shawn Kemp** 1989–1997 959	
ASSISTS	**Gary Payton** 7,384	**THREES**	**Rashard Lewis** 1998–2007 973	→

Hot from the Start

Kevin Durant didn't take long to find his place in the NBA. After his freshman year at the University of Texas, he was drafted second overall in 2007 by the SuperSonics. Averaging 20.3 points in his first season, he was named the 2007–2008 Rookie of the Year. Durant's success continued the following year, when he averaged 25.3 points per game. He broke out in 2009–2010, when he led the NBA with 30.1 points per game and led the Thunder to the playoffs.

Kevin Durant (35)

Sonics Legacy

When the SuperSonics left Seattle in 2008 for Oklahoma City to become the Thunder, basketball fans were left empty-handed. Although the Mariners of Major League Baseball and the Seahawks of the National Football League showed up to stay in the mid-1970s, Seattle fans still missed their Sonics. The NBA allowed Seattle to keep the SuperSonics nickname and green and gold colors in case the city can lure a new basketball team to town.

ORLANDO MAGIC

Franchise Record: 870–820
Home Arena: Amway Arena
(17,248 capacity) in Orlando, Florida

CHAMPIONSHIPS
None

First Season: 1989–1990

The Magic joined the NBA as an expansion team in 1989. The franchise landed young stars Shaquille O'Neal and Anfernee Hardaway in the 1992 and 1993 NBA drafts. By 1995 the Magic had made the playoffs but lost to the Houston Rockets in the Eastern Conference Finals. In 2009 the Magic went to the finals behind center Dwight Howard, but they lost to the Los Angeles Lakers.

Jameer Nelson (14) takes a jumper during the 2009 Finals.

Legends & Stars

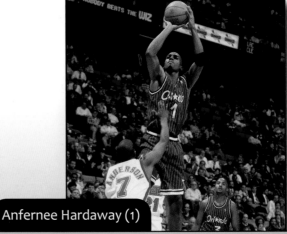
Anfernee Hardaway (1)

Nick Anderson	G	1989–1999	The all-time leading scorer in Magic history was with the team from the start
Anfernee Hardaway	G	1993–1999	"Penny" was on his way to becoming a superstar when knee injuries set him back
Dwight Howard	C	2004–present	"Superman" dominates opponents by swiping the glass clean of rebounds and tossing down forceful dunks
Jameer Nelson	G	2004–present	A quick-moving point guard, Nelson weaves his way around the court on both offense and defense
Shaquille O'Neal	C	1992–1996	The "Shaq Attack" played in four All-Star Games with the Magic; he led the league in scoring in the 1994–1995 season

By the Numbers

POINTS — **Nick Anderson** 1989–1999 10,650

STEALS — **Nick Anderson** 1,004

REBOUNDS — **Dwight Howard** 2004–present 6,189

BLOCKS — **Dwight Howard** 1,042

ASSISTS — **Scott Skiles** 1989–1994 2,776

THREES — **Dennis Scott** 1990–1997 981

Making Magic

Orlando was chosen as a site for NBA franchise expansion in 1989. When it came time to choose a name, team officials and the *Orlando Sentinel* sponsored a naming contest. From 4,296 entries the list was narrowed to Heat, Tropics, Juice, and Magic. Orlando—a tourist destination with Disney World, the Magic Kingdom, and more—was the perfect fit for "Magic."

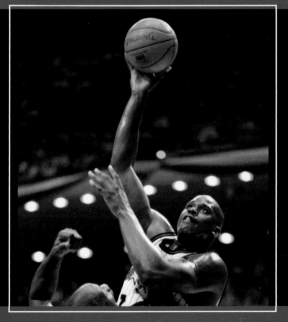

Lottery Luck

In 1991–1992 the Magic finished with the second-worst record in the NBA (21–61). However, they won the NBA draft lottery, which allowed them to select college star Shaquille O'Neal (left). The big center helped turn the team around, and the Magic ended with a 41–41 record in 1993. They won the draft lottery again that year, picking forward Chris Webber and trading him for guard Anfernee "Penny" Hardaway and several other players. With Penny and Shaq, the Magic made it to the NBA Finals two seasons later.

PHILADELPHIA 76ERS

First Season: 1949–1950

Franchise Record: 2,569–2,259
Home Arena: Wachovia Center (21,600 capacity) in Philadelphia, Pennsylvania

CHAMPIONSHIPS
1955, 1967, 1983

The Syracuse Reds formed an independent professional team in 1939 before renaming themselves the Syracuse Nationals and joining the National Basketball League in 1946. In 1949 the Nats joined the NBA and won the title in 1955. The team moved to Philadelphia in 1963 and changed to the 76ers. The Sixers took home NBA titles in 1967 and 1983 behind the talents of Julius "Dr. J." Erving and Moses Malone.

Andre Iguodala (9)

Legends & Stars

Julius Erving

Charles Barkley	F	1984–1992	Barkley went to the All-Star game five times as a 76er
Maurice Cheeks	G	1978–1989	Cheeks guided Philly to the NBA title in 1983 and later became the 76ers' coach for four seasons
Julius Erving	F	1976–1987	"Dr. J" was one of the best high-flying, slam-dunking players in the game; he was the NBA MVP in 1981
Hal Greer	F	1958–1973	The franchise's career leader in games played and points was a key member of the NBA title winners of 1967
Andre Iguodala	G/F	2004–present	Iguodala is known for his soaring jams, quick drives to the basket, and ability to steal the ball
Allen Iverson	G	1996–2006, 2010	"The Answer" led the NBA in scoring four times and won the 2001 MVP award

By the Numbers

POINTS	**Hal Greer** 1958–1973 21,586	
REBOUNDS	**Dolph Schayes** 1949–1964 11,256	
ASSISTS	**Maurice Cheeks** 1978–1989 6,212	
STEALS	**Maurice Cheeks** 1,942	
BLOCKS	**Julius Erving** 1976–1987 1,293	
THREES	**Allen Iverson** 1996–2006, 2010 885	→

Patriotic Name

The Syracuse Nationals came to town one year after Philadelphia lost its pro hoops team, the Warriors, in 1962. Team owners, in deciding to rename the franchise, went with the 76ers. It honored the year 1776, when America's Founding Fathers signed the Declaration of Independence in Philadelphia.

Moses Malone (2), 1983 Finals

Fo, Fo, Fo

Coming off a season in which they lost 4–2 in the 1982 NBA Finals, the Philadelphia 76ers wanted revenge. An offseason trade brought center Moses Malone to the team, and the next season was a big improvement. The Sixers ran over the competition during the 1982–1983 regular season. When Malone was asked how his team would do in the upcoming playoffs, Malone responded, "Fo, fo, fo," meaning they would sweep opponents four games in a row, three times. He wasn't far off: The Sixers lost only one game in the playoffs on their title run.

PHOENIX SUNS

First Season: 1968–1969

Franchise Record: 1,914–1,498
Home Arena: US Airways Center
(18,422 capacity) in Phoenix, Arizona

CHAMPIONSHIPS
None

In 1968 the NBA added two expansion teams: the Phoenix Suns and the Milwaukee Bucks. The Suns lost a coin flip to the Bucks to draft immensely talented center Kareem Abdul-Jabbar, but the team slowly built a winner. In 1976 the Suns made their first NBA Finals but lost to the Boston Celtics. The Suns blazed to the NBA Finals again in 1993 behind the play of forward Charles Barkley before losing to the Chicago Bulls.

The Phoenix Suns during a pre-game huddle at US Airways Center

Legends & Stars

Amare Stoudemire (1)

Walter Davis	F	1977–1988	High-scoring Davis was the 1977–1978 Rookie of the Year and went on to become a six-time NBA All-Star
Kevin Johnson	G	1988–2000	Surprisingly strong for a point guard, "KJ" put the Suns on his back for many seasons during a legendary career
Dan Majerle	G	1988–1995, 2001–2002	"Thunder Dan" had a shooting range that almost extended to half-court; he made the NBA All-Defensive Team twice
Steve Nash	G	1996–1998, 2004–present	The fast-footed Nash can knock down threes and has a knack for getting the ball to teammates
Amare Stoudemire	F	2002–present	The 2002–2003 Rookie of the Year is a five-time All-Star

By the Numbers

POINTS
Walter Davis
1977–1988
15,666

STEALS
Alvan Adams
1,289

REBOUNDS
Alvan Adams
1975–1988
6,937

BLOCKS
Larry Nance
1981–1988
940

ASSISTS
Kevin Johnson
1988–2000
6,518

THREES
Steve Nash
1996–1998, 2004–present
915 ⟶

Triple the Fun

In Game 5 of the 1976 NBA Finals, the Suns played the Boston Celtics in what many consider to be the greatest game in NBA history. With the series tied 2–2, the Suns were down 22 points but fought back to put the game into overtime, and then double overtime, and then triple overtime. When the dust settled, the Celtics had escaped with a 128-126 victory. The Suns couldn't bounce back during the next game, and the Celtics took home the championship.

Outdoor Fun

The Suns became the first team in modern-day NBA history to play outdoors. On October 11, 2008, they took on the Denver Nuggets in a preseason game in Indian Wells, California. Playing in an outdoor stadium designed for tennis, the Suns downed the Nuggets 77-72. The two teams combined to miss 24 of 27 three-pointers—probably because of the gusting winds and cool temperatures.

PORTLAND TRAIL BLAZERS

First Season: 1970–1971

Franchise Record: 1,733–1,515
Home Arena: Rose Garden Arena
(19,980 capacity) in Portland, Oregon

CHAMPIONSHIP
1977

The Trail Blazers started out as an NBA expansion team in 1970. In 1974 the Blazers picked up do-it-all center Bill Walton in the NBA draft, and "Blazermania" soon swept through the Pacific Northwest. Walton led the Blazers to the 1977 NBA title over the heavily favored Philadelphia 76ers. Smooth guard Clyde Drexler led Portland on the court throughout much of the 1980s and into the 1990s.

Greg Oden (52) got off to a slow start in the NBA because of injuries.

Legends & Stars

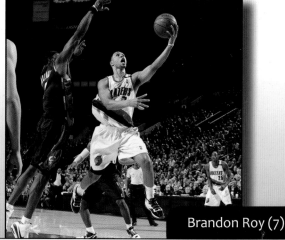
Brandon Roy (7)

Clyde Drexler	F	1983–1995	"Clyde the Glide" was an eight-time All-Star with the Blazers; he was inducted into the Hall of Fame in 2004
Maurice Lucas	F	1976–1980, 1987–1988	Lucas was one of the game's fiercest rebounders and scorers for the 1977 NBA champs
Terry Porter	G	1985–1995	Porter led the Trail Blazers to the finals in 1990 and 1992
Brandon Roy	G	2006–present	The 2006–2007 Rookie of the Year has already been to three All-Star games
Bill Walton	C	1974–1978	Considered one of the best centers in history, Walton began his NBA career in Portland

By the Numbers

POINTS	**Clyde Drexler** 1983–1995 18,040	**STEALS**	**Clyde Drexler** 1,795 →	
REBOUNDS	**Clyde Drexler** 5,339	**BLOCKS**	**Mychal Thompson** 1978–1979, 1980–1986 768	
ASSISTS	**Terry Porter** 1985–1995 5,319	**THREES**	**Terry Porter** 773	

Blazermania

Portland finished the 1975–1976 season in last place in their division, but the next season was a new beginning. Led by center Bill Walton and new arrivals John Lucas and coach Jack Ramsay, the Blazers won over fans with a 49–33 regular season. Their team-oriented play led them to the NBA championship. A big part of the Blazers' success was the support from their fans, who nicknamed themselves "Blazermaniacs."

Bill Walton (32)

Short but Sweet

As a 22-year-old guard from Princeton University in 1970, Geoff Petrie took the league by storm as a member of the Blazers. His first year he averaged 24.8 points per game and captured the Rookie of the Year award. By Petrie's third season, he was lighting up the scoreboards, twice scorching the Houston Rockets for more than 50 points. The success stopped short after a knee injury ended his playing career in 1976. Petrie became a basketball executive for the Blazers and, later, the Sacramento Kings.

SACRAMENTO KINGS

First Season: 1948–1949

Franchise Record: 2,300–2,593
Home Arena: Arco Arena
(17,317 capacity) in Sacramento, California

CHAMPIONSHIP
1951

The team got its start in 1945 in the National Basketball League as the Rochester Royals. The ballclub switched to the Basketball Association of America in 1948 before joining the NBA in 1949. The Royals were based in Cincinnati from 1957 to 1972, and then moved west. They were named the Kings and split their time between two NBA cities—Kansas City and Omaha. They officially settled in Kansas City in 1975, and in 1985 the Kings packed up and moved even farther west—to Sacramento.

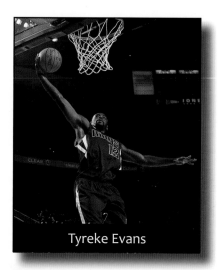
Tyreke Evans

Legends & Stars

Kevin Martin (23)

Nate Archibald	G	1970–1976	During the 1972–1973 season, "Tiny" became the first player to lead the NBA in both scoring and assists
Tyreke Evans	G	2009–present	The former University of Memphis guard always finds a way to the rim
Kevin Martin	F	2004–2010	With a dangerous side-winding three-point shot, Martin carried the Kings' offense for more than five seasons
Mitch Richmond	F	1991–1998	Richmond was one of the Kings' leading scorers
Oscar Robertson	G	1960–1970	"The Big O" was a great all-around player who was inducted into the Hall of Fame in 1980
Chris Webber	F	1998–2005	The five-time NBA All-Star was a double-double machine

By the Numbers

POINTS	Oscar Robertson 1960–1970 22,009	**STEALS**	Sam Lacey 950	
REBOUNDS	Sam Lacey 1970–1981 9,353	**BLOCKS**	Sam Lacey 1,098	
ASSISTS	Oscar Robertson 7,731	**THREES**	Peja Stojakovic 1998–2006 1,070	

Royal Name

When the basketball Royals moved to Kansas City in 1972, a name change was in order. The Royals name was already taken by the Kansas City major league baseball team. The Royals became the Kings and kept their noble name when they moved to Sacramento, California, in 1985.

The Title That Got Away

The Kings finished the 2001–2002 regular season at 61–21. They were a favorite to win the NBA title. In the playoffs they stormed their way to the Western Conference Finals, where they battled the Los Angeles Lakers in a hard-fought series. Game 7 was a heartbreaker for Sacramento fans, with the Kings shooting just 2-for-20 from three-point range and 16-for-30 from the foul line. Even with the poor shooting, they forced the game into overtime but eventually lost 112-106.

Chris Webber (4) led the Kings to the league's best record in 2001–2002.

SAN ANTONIO SPURS

First Season: 1967–1968

Franchise Record: 2,031–1,469
Home Arena: AT&T Center
(18,797 capacity) in San Antonio, Texas

CHAMPIONSHIPS
1999, 2003, 2005, 2007

One of the original American Basketball Association franchises, the Dallas Chaparrals played six seasons in Dallas before moving to San Antonio and becoming the Spurs. In 1976 the Spurs were one of four ABA teams to move to the NBA. Guard George Gervin entertained fans with his famous finger-roll flip for more than a decade. In 1999, behind skilled big men David Robinson and Tim Duncan, the Spurs won their first NBA title, and three more followed in the 2000s.

2007 NBA champions

Legends & Stars

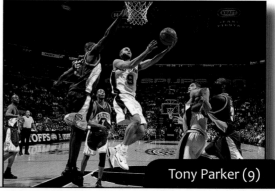

Tony Parker (9)

Tim Duncan	F	1993–present	The backbone of four NBA championship teams, Duncan is a two-time MVP and a 12-time All-Star
Sean Elliott	F	1989–1993, 1994–2001	Elliott was a clutch shooter who became the first NBA player to play after a kidney transplant
George Gervin	G	1974–1985	The "Iceman" received nine NBA All-Star selections and three from the ABA
Manu Ginobili	G	2002–present	The quick guard has helped his team to three NBA titles
Avery Johnson	G	1991, 1992–1993, 1994–2001	"The Little General" propelled the Spurs to their first NBA title from his point guard position
Tony Parker	G	2001–present	One of the fastest players in the NBA led San Antonio to three championships
David Robinson	C	1989–2003	"The Admiral" won three NBA titles and the 1995 MVP award

By the Numbers

POINTS	George Gervin 1974–1985 23,602	**STEALS**	David Robinson 1989–2003 1,388
REBOUNDS	Tim Duncan 1993–present 11,335	**BLOCKS**	David Robinson 2,954
ASSISTS	Avery Johnson 1991, 1992–1993, 1994–2001 4,474	**THREES**	Manu Ginobili 2002–present 804

Twin Towers

The effective combo of 7-foot (213-centimeter) stars David Robinson and Tim Duncan may have been the best one-two punch under the basket. Playing together for six seasons from 1997 to 2003, the duo helped San Antonio to championships in 1999 and 2003.

Tim Duncan (21) and David Robinson

Winning Ways

Along with the Spurs, the Indiana Pacers, New York Nets, and Denver Nuggets joined the NBA in 1976. The Spurs found quick success in the new league, capturing division titles in five of their first six NBA seasons. In 2003 the Spurs met the New Jersey Nets in the NBA Finals—the first time the championship was played between former ABA teams.

TORONTO RAPTORS

First Season: 1995–1996

Franchise Record: 502–696
Home Arena: Air Canada Centre
(19,800 capacity) in Toronto, Ontario, Canada

CHAMPIONSHIPS
None

In 1946 the Toronto Huskies became one of the original teams of the Basketball Association of America. But when the Huskies flamed out after a single season, Toronto basketball fans would have to wait until 1995 for their next pro team. The Raptors were added as part of an NBA expansion along with the Vancouver Grizzlies. Guard Vince Carter was one of the Raptors' first superstars. In 2001 he led Toronto to the second round of the playoffs for the first time in franchise history.

Chris Bosh (4)

Legends & Stars

Tracy McGrady (1)

Chris Bosh	F/C	2003–present	The high-scoring post player was selected to five consecutive All-Star games between 2006 and 2010
Vince Carter	G	1998–2004	For six and a half seasons in Toronto, Carter led the team in scoring
Tracy McGrady	F	1997–2000	McGrady grew up with the Raptors and had transformed into a dominant star after he left Toronto
Damon Stoudamire	G	1995–1998	The first NBA draft pick in Raptors' franchise history, "Mighty Mouse" was a quick player with scoring and passing skills

By the Numbers

POINTS	**Vince Carter** 1998–2004 9,420		**STEALS**	**Doug Christie** 1996–2000 664
REBOUNDS	**Chris Bosh** 2003–present 4,776		**BLOCKS**	**Chris Bosh** 600
ASSISTS	**Jose Calderon** 2005–present 2,364		**THREES**	**Morris Peterson** 2000–2007 801

It Pays to Be Tall

The first game in the BAA was played November 1, 1946. The Toronto Huskies took on the New York Knickerbockers at Maple Leaf Gardens in Toronto. As a promotion the team gave free admission to any fan taller than the Huskies' center George Nostrand (6 feet 8 inches; 203 centimeters). Toronto lost an exciting game to New York, 68-66.

Turnaround in Toronto

After finishing with the fifth-worst record in the NBA during the 2005–2006 season, the team hired Bryan Colangelo, the 2004–2005 NBA Executive of the Year, as GM and president. The Raptors took Andrea Bargnani with the first overall pick of the draft and traded for point guard T.J. Ford. After a mediocre start, the Raptors finished 45–37 and led their division. They were seeded third in the playoffs, but they fell to the New Jersey Nets 4–2 in the first round.

Andrea Bargnani (7)

UTAH JAZZ

Franchise Record: 1,594–1,326
Home Arena: EnergySolutions Arena
(19,991 capacity) in Salt Lake City, Utah

CHAMPIONSHIPS
None

First Season: 1974–1975

The New Orleans Jazz were born when the NBA expanded in 1974. Dazzling guard Pete Maravich was acquired in a trade, but an unlucky knee injury in 1978 ended his career and New Orleans' hopes for success. The Jazz moved to Utah but kept their nickname as new stars John Stockton and Karl Malone arrived in the mid-1980s. Utah challenged the Chicago Bulls for the NBA title in 1997 and 1998, but they came up short both times.

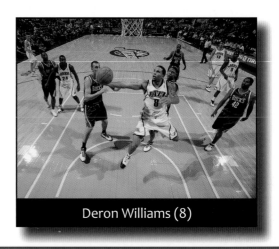
Deron Williams (8)

Legends & Stars

John Stockton (12)

Carlos Boozer	F/C	2004–present	High-scoring rebound machine has been to two All-Star games
Mark Eaton	C	1982–1993	A giant under the basket, Eaton was a big part of turning the franchise around in the 1980s
Jeff Hornacek	F/G	1994–2000	One of the steadiest players in the league in the 1990s, Hornacek was a world-class shooter from the perimeter
Karl Malone	F	1985–2003	In his 18 seasons at power forward for the Jazz, Malone was a 14-time All-Star and the NBA's MVP in 1997 and 1999
Pete Maravich	G	1974–1980	"Pistol Pete" played seven seasons at shooting guard for the Jazz; he scored a franchise-record 68 points in a game in 1977
John Stockton	G	1984–2003	One of the NBA's greatest point guards holds the league's career assists and steals records
Deron Williams	G	2005–present	Williams, one of the best NBA point guards, was a 2010 All-Star

By the Numbers

POINTS	Karl Malone 1985–2003 36,374	**STEALS**	John Stockton 3,265
REBOUNDS	Karl Malone 14,601	**BLOCKS**	Mark Eaton 1982–1993 3,064
ASSISTS	John Stockton 1984–2003 15,806	**THREES**	John Stockton 845

Music in the Mountains

Though the Jazz seems like an odd name for a basketball club from Utah, the name started in New Orleans, a city well-known for its jazz music. The team played just five seasons there, but there was no desire to change the name when it moved to Salt Lake City. The Jazz have played well for the fans in their new home over the years. The team made the playoffs every season from 1984 to 2003. After three mediocre seasons, the Jazz returned to the playoffs each year from 2007 to 2010.

Sideline Stability

In an era where coaches quickly come and go, Jerry Sloan of the Jazz has stood out. Once a scrappy, hustling guard for the Chicago Bulls, Sloan brought a similar intensity to the bench. He coached the Bulls for three years starting in 1979 before signing on with the Jazz in 1988. Still pacing the Utah sidelines in 2009–2010, his 22nd season with the Jazz, Sloan was inducted into the Basketball Hall of Fame in 2009 for his coaching skills.

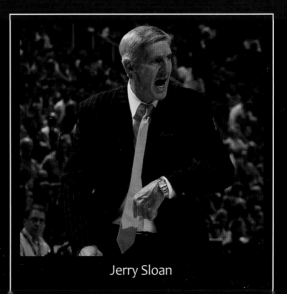

Jerry Sloan

WASHINGTON WIZARDS

First Season: 1961–1962

Franchise Record: 1,801–2,174
Home Arena: Verizon Center
(20,173 capacity) in Washington, D.C.

CHAMPIONSHIP
1978

The Wizards franchise started in 1961 as the Chicago Packers in the NBA. The next season they changed to the Zephyrs for one year before moving to Baltimore and becoming the Bullets. The Bullets moved on to Washington, D.C., in 1973 and were briefly called the Capitol Bullets. They became the Washington Bullets in 1974 and won the NBA title in 1978 behind team captain Wes Unseld. In 1997 the team was renamed once again, this time as the Wizards.

Andray Blatche (7)

Legends & Stars

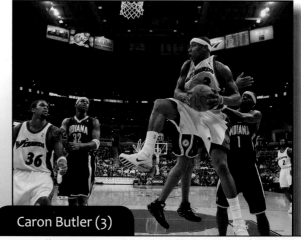
Caron Butler (3)

Caron Butler	F	2005–2010	The two-time All-Star was a threat on both ends of the court
Elvin Hayes	F	1972–1981	"The Big E" was a 12-time NBA All-Star who went to the playoffs six times as a Bullet
Gus Johnson	F/C	1963–1972	"Honeycomb" was a five-time NBA All-Star who averaged a double-double in points and rebounds for his career
Michael Jordan	G	2001–2003	MJ averaged 20-plus points per game and topped 40 points in a game eight times for Washington in the last years of his career
Wes Unseld	C	1968–1981	Unseld was named the NBA's Rookie of the Year and MVP in 1968–1969

By the Numbers

POINTS	**Elvin Hayes** 1972–1981 15,551	**STEALS**	**Greg Ballard** 1977–1985 762
REBOUNDS	**Wes Unseld** 1968–1981 13,769	**BLOCKS**	**Elvin Hayes** 1,558 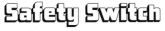
ASSISTS	**Wes Unseld** 3,822	**THREES**	**Gilbert Arenas** 2003–present 821

Safety Switch

In 1995 owner Abe Pollan decided he needed to change his team name from the Bullets to something less violent. With support from the fans, Washington, D.C.'s basketball team became known as the Wizards in the 1997–1998 season.

Tall and Talented

At 7 feet 7 inches (226 centimeters) tall, Romanian Gheorghe Muresan shared the honor of tallest NBA player with Manute Bol from Sudan. When Muresan was selected by the Bullets in the 1993 NBA draft, many doubted he'd make an impact in the league. But by his third season, Muresan averaged 14.5 points, 9.6 rebounds, and 2.3 blocks per game while making 58.4 percent of his shots—the top mark in the league. Though injuries plagued his career, he remains the most accurate shooter in Washington Wizards franchise history with a career 57.8 percentage in four seasons with the club.

Gheorghe Muresan (77)

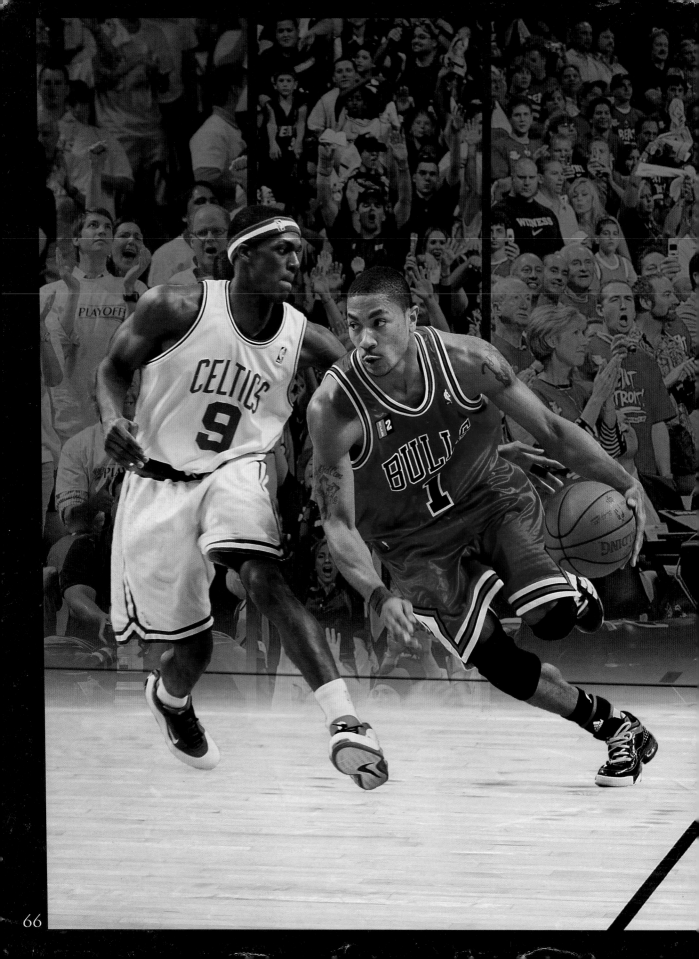

Portland
Trail Blazers

Sacramento Kings

Golden State
Warriors

Utah Jazz

Denver Nuggets

Los Angeles Clippers
Los Angeles Lakers

Oklahoma City
Thunder

Phoenix Suns

Dallas Mavericks

San Antonio Spurs

TEAM
MAP

Minnesota Timberwolves

Toronto Raptors

Boston Celtics

Milwaukee Bucks

Detroit Pistons

New York Knicks New Jersey Nets

Chicago Bulls

Cleveland Cavaliers

Philadelphia 76ers

Indiana Pacers

Washington Wizards

Charlotte Bobcats

Memphis Grizzlies

Atlanta Hawks

New Orleans Hornets

Houston Rockets

Orlando Magic

Miami Heat

GLOSSARY

baseline—area running along the out-of-bounds line under each basket

clutch—describes a player who performs well during crucial moments of the game

double-double—reaching double figures in two categories in a single game, such as scoring 10 or more points and getting 10 or more rebounds

expansion team—a new team that is added to the professional league

paint—the rectangular area marked by a large rectangle directly under the basket and extending to the free-throw line; the area is often painted a different color from the rest of the court

post—the area around the basket, generally within a 10-foot (3-meter) radius, where the center or forwards "post up" and try to get open to receive a pass

triple-double—reaching double figures in three categories in a single game; usually achieved in points, rebounds, and assists

BASKETBALL POSITIONS

center (C)—position of a player who plays mostly near the basket; this player is often the tallest and biggest on the team

forward (F)—position of a player who plays both inside and outside; the players in this position are often skilled at scoring on offense in a variety of ways

guard (G)—position of a player who plays mostly on the perimeter; this player is often one of the quicker players on the team who can dribble and pass well

point guard (PG)—type of guard who brings the ball up the court and is a good passer

power forward (PF)—type of forward who is next in size behind the center; spends most of the time in the post

shooting guard (SG)—type of guard who can shoot from the perimeter and is relied on for scoring

small forward (SF)—type of forward who is balanced in scoring, defending, and passing; the small forward usually has the speed to play on the perimeter and the size to play in the post

READ MORE

Christopher, Matt. *Great Moments in Basketball History.* New York: Little, Brown Books for Young Readers, 2009.

Doeden, Matt. *The World's Greatest Basketball Players.* Mankato, Minn.: Capstone Press, 2010.

Shea, Therese. *Basketball Stars.* New York: Children's Press, 2007.

Wyckoff, Edwin Brit. *The Man Who Invented Basketball: James Naismith and His Amazing Game.* Berkeley Heights, N.J.: Enslow Publishers, 2008.

INTERNET SITES

FactHound offers a safe, fun way to find Internet sites related to this book. All of the sites on FactHound have been researched by our staff.

Here's all you do:

Visit *www.facthound.com*

Type in this code: 9781429648219

INDEX

Abdul-Jabbar, Kareem, 30, 31, 36, 37, 52
Abdur-Rahim, Shareef, 32
Adams, Alvan, 53
Aguirre, Mark, 16
Alcindor, Lew. See Abdul-Jabbar, Kareem.
Allen, Ray, 9, 37
Anderson, Nick, 48, 49
Anthony, Carmelo, 18
Archibald, Nate, 56
Arenas, Gilbert, 65
Arizin, Paul, 22

Ballard, Greg, 65
Bargnani, Andrea, 61
Barkley, Charles, 50, 52
Barnett, Dick, 45
Barry, Rick, 22
Battier, Shane, 33
Baylor, Elgin, 30, 31
Beasley, Michael, 34
Beck, Byron, 18
Benjamin, Benoit, 29
Bird, Larry, 5, 8, 9, 26, 27
Blackman, Rolando, 16
Blatche, Andray, 64
Blaylock, Mookie, 7
Boe, Roy, 41
Bogues, Muggsy, 42, 43
Bogut, Andrew, 36
Bol, Manute, 65
Boozer, Carlos, 62
Bosh, Chris, 60, 61
Bowman, Nate, 45
Bradley, Bill, 44, 45
Bradley, Shawn, 17
Brand, Elton, 29
Brooks, Aaron, 24
Brown, Freddie, 46
Brown, Hubie, 33
Brown, P.J., 43
Bryant, Kobe, 30, 31
Buckner, Quinn, 37
Butler, Caron, 64
Bynum, Andrew, 31

Calderon, Jose, 61
Carr, Austin, 14
Carter, Don, 17
Carter, Vince, 60, 61
Chamberlain, Wilt, 4, 22, 23, 31
Cheeks, Maurice, 50, 51
Christie, Doug, 61
Colangelo, Bryan, 61
Coleman, Derrick, 40
Cooper, Michael, 31

Cousy, Bob, 4, 8, 9
Cuban, Mark, 17
Curry, Dell, 42, 43
Curry, Stephen, 22

Dandridge, Bob, 36
Daniels, Mel, 27
Daugherty, Brad, 14, 15
Davis, Brad, 16
Davis, Jefferson, 7
Davis, Walter, 52, 53
Dawkins, Darryl, 40
DeBusschere, Dave, 45
Drexler, Clyde, 25, 54, 55
Dumars, Joe, 20, 21
Duncan, Tim, 58, 59
Durant, Kevin, 46, 47

Eaton, Mark, 62, 63
Elliott, Sean, 58
Ellis, Monta, 22
English, Alex, 18, 19
Erving, Julius, 5, 40, 41, 50, 51
Evans, Tyreke, 56
Ewing, Patrick, 44, 45

Felton, Raymond, 10, 11
Finley, Michael, 16
Ford, T.J., 61
Foyle, Adonal, 23
Frazier, Walt, 44, 45

Gallinari, Danilo, 44
Garner, James, 17
Garnett, Kevin, 9, 38, 39
Gasol, Pau, 32, 33
Gay, Rudy, 32
Gervin, George, 58, 59
Gianelli, John, 45
Gibson, Daniel, 14
Gilmore, Artis, 12, 13
Ginobili, Manu, 58, 59
Gordon, Eric, 28
Granger, Danny, 26
Green, A.C., 31
Greer, Hal, 50, 51
Griffin, Blake, 29
Gugliotta, Tom, 38

Hamilton, Richard, 20
Hardaway, Anfernee, 48, 49
Hardaway, Tim, 34, 35
Harper, Derek, 17
Harper, Ron, 15
Harris, Devin, 40
Havlicek, John, 8, 9
Haywood, Spencer, 46

Hayes, Elvin, 64, 65
Henderson, Gerald, 10
Hinrich, Kirk, 13
Holzman, William, 45
Horford, Al, 7
Hornacek, Jeff, 62
Howard, Dwight, 5, 48, 49
Hudson, Lou, 6

Iguodala, Andre, 50
Ilgauskas, Zydrunas, 14, 15
Irving, Washington, 45
Issel, Dan, 18, 19
Iverson, Allen, 50, 51

Jackson, Mark, 26
Jackson, Phil, 45
Jackson, Stephen, 11
James, LeBron, 5, 14, 15
Jennings, Brandon, 36
Johnson, Avery, 58, 59
Johnson, Earvin, 5, 30, 31
Johnson, George, 41
Johnson, Gus, 64
Johnson, Joe, 6
Johnson, Kevin, 52, 53
Johnson, Larry, 42
Johnson, Robert, 11
Jordan, Michael, 5, 11, 12, 13, 20, 64

Kaman, Chris, 28
Karl, George, 19
Kemp, Shawn, 46, 47
Kidd, Jason, 40, 41

Lacey, Sam, 57
Laimbeer, Bill, 20, 21
Lang, John, 21
Lanier, Bob, 20
Lever, Lafayette, 18, 19
Lewis, Rashard, 47
Lincoln, Abraham, 7
Listner, Alton, 37
Love, Bob, 12
Love, Kevin, 38
Lucas, John, 55
Lucas, Maurice, 54

Mahorn, Rick, 21
Majerle, Dan, 52
Malone, Karl, 62, 63
Malone, Moses, 50, 51
Manning, Danny, 28
Maravich, Pete, 5, 6, 62
Marbury, Stephon, 39
Martin, Kevin, 56
Maxwell, Vernon, 25
Mayo, O.J., 32
McAdoo, Bob, 28
McGinnis, George, 26
McGrady, Tracy, 60
Meminger, Dean, 45

Mikan, George, 30
Miller, Mike, 33
Miller, Reggie, 26, 27
Ming, Yao, 24
Mitchell, Sam, 38
Moe, Doug, 19
Moncrief, Sidney, 36
Monroe, Earl, 44, 45
Mourning, Alonzo, 34, 35, 42, 43
Mullin, Chris, 22, 23
Muresan, Gheorghe, 65
Murphy, Calvin, 24, 25
Mutombo, Dikembe, 6, 19

Naismith, James, 4
Nance, Larry, 53
Nash, Steve, 52, 53
Nelson, Jameer, 48
Nostrand, George, 61
Nowitzki, Dirk, 16, 17

Oden, Greg, 54
Okafor, Emeka, 10, 11
Olajuwon, Hakeem, 24, 25
O'Neal, Jermaine, 27
O'Neal, Shaquille, 31, 34, 35, 48, 49

Parish, Robert, 8, 9
Parker, Tony, 58
Paul, Chris, 42
Payton, Gary, 46, 47
Peeler, Anthony, 39
Peterson, Morris, 61
Petrie, Geoff, 55
Pettit, Bob, 4, 6, 7
Piatkowski, Eric, 29
Pierce, Paul, 8, 9
Pippen, Scottie, 12
Pollan, Abe, 65
Porter, Terry, 54, 55
Pressey, Paul, 37
Price, Mark, 14, 15
Prince, Tayshaun, 20

Rambis, Kurt, 31
Ramsay, Jack, 55
Reed, Willis, 44, 45
Reeves, Bryant, 32
Rice, Glen, 34
Richardson, Jason, 23
Richmond, Mitch, 56
Riley, Pat, 34
Rivers, Glenn, 7
Robertson, Oscar, 36, 56, 57
Robinson, David, 58, 59
Robinson, Glenn, 36
Robinzine, Bill, 41
Rodgers, Guy, 23
Rodman, Dennis, 21
Rollins, Tree, 7

Rondo, Rajon, 8
Rose, Derrick, 12
Roy, Brandon, 54
Russell, Bill, 4, 8, 9

Schayes, Dolph, 51
Scott, Byron, 31
Scott, Dennis, 49
Sealy, Malik, 39
Seikaly, Rony, 34
Sikma, Jack, 46, 47
Skiles, Scott, 49
Sloan, Jerry, 12, 63
Smith, Bingo, 14
Smith, Josh, 6
Smith, J.R., 19
Smith, Randy, 28, 29
Smits, Rik, 26
Sonju, Norm, 17
Stallworth, Dave, 45
Starks, John, 27, 45
Stockton, John, 62, 63
Stojakovic, Peja, 57
Stoudamire, Damon, 60
Stoudemire, Amare, 52
Szczerbiak, Wally, 38

Terry, Jason, 16
Thomas, Isiah, 20, 21
Thompson, David, 18
Thompson, Mychal, 55
Thurmond, Nate, 22, 23
Tomjanovich, Rudy, 24
Tripucka, Kelly, 21

Unseld, Wes, 64, 65

Wade, Dwyane, 34, 35
Wallace, Ben, 20, 21
Wallace, Gerald, 10, 11
Walton, Bill, 28, 54, 55
Webber, Chris, 49, 56, 57
West, David, 42
West, Jerry, 30
Westbrook, Russell, 46
Wilkins, Dominique, 6, 7
Williams, Buck, 40, 41
Williams, Deron, 62
Williams, Jason, 33
Williams, John, 15
Wingo, Harthorne, 45
Worthy, James, 31
Wright, Lorenzen, 32

Zollner, Fred, 20